THE EXTRAORDINARY LIFE OF

KATHERINE
JOHNSON

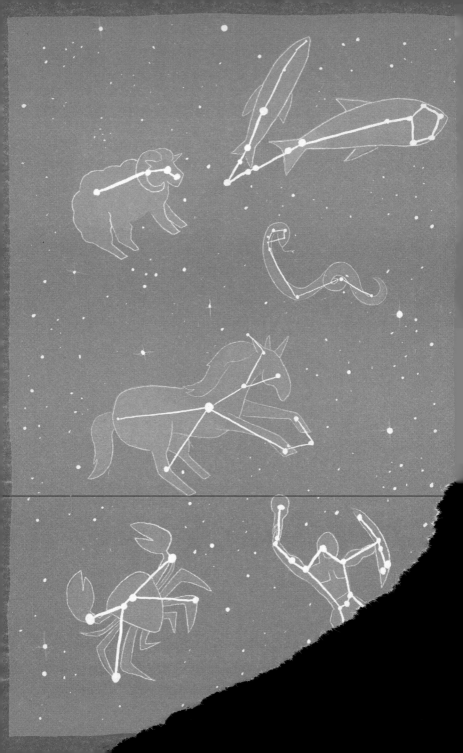

PUFFIN BOOKS

UK | USA | Canada | Ireland | Australia
India | New Zealand | South Africa

Puffin Books is part of the Penguin Random House group of companies
whose addresses can be found at global.penguinrandomhouse.com.

www.penguin.co.uk
www.puffin.co.uk
www.ladybird.co.uk

Penguin
Random House
UK

First published 2019

001

Text design by Mandy Norman
Printed and bound by CPI Group (UK) Ltd, Croydon, CR0 4YY

A CIP catalogue record for this book is available from the British Library

ISBN: 978–0–241–37544–0

All correspondence to:
Puffin Books, Penguin Random House Children's
80 Strand, London WC2R 0RL

MIX
Paper from
responsible sources
FSC® C018179

Penguin Random House is committed to a
sustainable future for our business, our readers
and our planet. This book is made from Forest
Stewardship Council® certified paper.

THE EXTRAORDINARY LIFE OF

KATHERINE
JOHNSON

Written by Devika Jina
Illustrated by Maggie Cole

EXTRAORDINARY LIVES
PUFFIN

United States of America

WEST
VIRGINIA

INSTITUTE

VIRGINIA

NASA
LANGLEY
RESEARCH
CENTER

MARION

WHITE
SULPHUR
SPRINGS

FLORIDA

KENNEDY
SPACE
CENTER

WHO IS
Katherine Johnson?

Katherine Johnson

was born on 26 August 1918 in White Sulphur Springs
in the state of West Virginia, America.

Katherine was **talented** beyond her years. She started high school at just ten years old (three years earlier than normal) and she *graduated* from college (university) at eighteen. Katherine achieved great things from a very young age, and at a time when few black people had the opportunity to gain a high-school diploma.

In 1953 Katherine started working at the Langley Research Center, which was part of what we now know as NASA. Here, Katherine was hired to work out complicated *mathematical problems*. Katherine aced this, and after only two weeks she was *promoted* to work on a new project where she discovered how planes and other aircraft move in the sky.

NASA:
the National Aeronautics and Space Administration, the US space agency. America's interest in space travel began in 1955, with the race against Russia to become the first country to send a person to space.

When America started competing with the USSR at *space travel*, Katherine showed how much she could accomplish.

USSR:
the name Russia used to be known by. America and the USSR both wanted to be the first country to send humans into space. USSR stands for the Union of Soviet Socialist Republics.

In 1961 an astronaut named **_Alan Shepard_** became the first American in space, but it was Katherine's **_calculations_** that got him there.

Katherine worked out the TRAJECTORY he would need to follow in order to get to space and arrive home safely.

$$\frac{W_1}{W_1 d}\frac{Y_d}{Y} = e^{\frac{W}{W}d + e^{\frac{2c_D}{c_L}}}$$

TRAJECTORY: path and direction.

Katherine continued to calculate the maths behind space missions, even after NASA started using **electronic computers**.

Katherine was no ordinary maths whizz, so she wasn't done shining just yet. Eight years later, in 1969, Neil Armstrong and Buzz Aldrin became the first men to **walk on the moon**, but Katherine was the woman who got them there and back.

DID YOU KNOW?

PROJECT APOLLO was the spaceflight programme that landed the first humans on the moon.

'I FELT
most proud
on the success
OF THE
Apollo
MISSION.'

Katherine has achieved so much in her life, never letting anything prevent her from learning, working and *discovering*.

The little girl who loved to count grew up to become the woman who sent people travelling to space, proving that if we work hard enough, we can *reach for the stars*.

Today Katherine lives in Hampton, Virginia, with her husband, James. Hers has been a **busy life**, and now she can look back at the incredible things she's achieved.

Katherine grew up, worked and lived at a time when black people in America were often **treated unfairly** compared to white people, so she faced **barriers** that could have stopped her. But she never let them stand in her way. This is her extraordinary story.

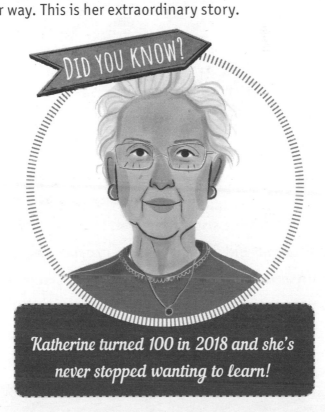

DID YOU KNOW?

Katherine turned 100 in 2018 and she's never stopped wanting to learn!

Katherine's beginnings

Katherine Coleman was born in White Sulphur Springs on 26 August 1918. Her mother, Joylette, was a teacher, and her father, Joshua, was a farmer, handyman and lumberjack.

Katherine had a happy childhood. The youngest of four children, she had two brothers, Horace and Charles, and one sister, Margaret. She was a **bright and curious** girl who grabbed every opportunity to learn something new. Joshua encouraged Katherine and made her believe in her abilities, never giving up on her. He was a great **role model** to Katherine.

'He always said, "YOU WILL GO TO COLLEGE." I didn't even know what a college was!'

Though Katherine loved learning about pretty much anything, it was **numbers** that really sparked her imagination. She became excited about maths from a very early age, fascinated by its *patterns and logic*.

She could see numbers anywhere. In all sorts of places, she'd be *counting* and smiling inside as she learned more and more.

5   11   8

16   14

12

1

'THE STEPS
TO THE ROAD,
the steps up to church,
THE NUMBER OF DISHES
ND SILVERWARE I WASHED . . .
anything that could be counted,
I DID.'

Katherine was so **keen to learn** that she would even follow her older brother Horace to school. Seeing this talented young girl and wanting to help her shine, Horace's teacher invited Katherine to summer school.

'I WAS ALWAYS
AROUND PEOPLE
WHO WERE
learning
something.
I LIKED TO LEARN.'

Katherine's brilliance impressed her teachers so much that she started high school at just **ten years old**. She was so smart that she even managed to skip ahead of some of her older siblings. However, Katherine stayed **humble** and did not allow this to affect her relationship with them.

For Katherine to attend high school, the family had to move 120 miles to the town of Institute, West Virginia. Her parents were ready to do **anything** to help their bright young daughter achieve all that they believed she could.

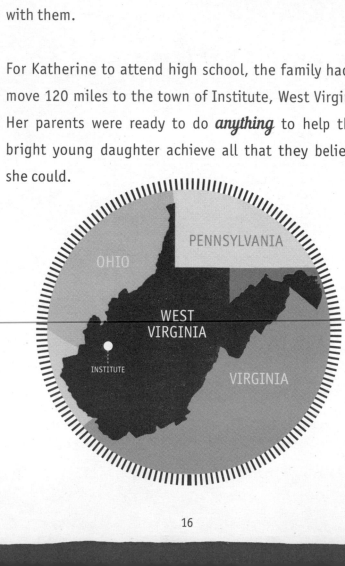

OHIO

PENNSYLVANIA

WEST
VIRGINIA

INSTITUTE

VIRGINIA

Thanks to her teacher Miss Turner, Katherine's love of numbers got stronger still when she first discovered GEOMETRY.

GEOMETRY:

the study of shapes, lines and angles. It was this that helped Katherine calculate how to get astronauts to and from space in one piece!

5

6

18

3

*A*fter finishing high school, Katherine was awarded a place at West Virginia State College.

Katherine grew up at a time when **RACIAL SEGREGATION** was still widespread.

RACIAL SEGREGATION: the act of forcing black people to use separate spaces from white people. Schools, universities and even buses were segregated at the time.

Schools for black children had **worse** classrooms, books and facilities compared to schools for white children. Black adults were only able to apply for jobs with **lower pay**, and even on buses black people had to sit on a small number of seats at the back.

At West Virginia State College Katherine needed to decide which subject would be her **major** (her main subject of study). She enjoyed English, French and maths, but she chose **French and maths**.

Katherine fondly remembers one of her professors jokingly saying:

'I'M COMING BACK TO TEACH *math this year*, AND IF YOU DON'T COME TO MY CLASS I'M GOING TO *come and find you*.'

She knew she had to pursue her love of numbers. But she also chose French because she loved it, and wasn't ready to stop learning it yet.

Katherine was also taught by **Dr William Claytor**, who was the third black man to earn a PHD in mathematics from an American university.

PHD:
an advanced, super-challenging degree that you might choose to do if you want to specialize in a particular subject. You do a lot of writing and teach others about your subject.

Dr Claytor told Katherine that if she worked hard enough and **believed** in herself, she could become a great research mathematician. He did everything he could to help. Katherine took every single one of his classes, and he even created a new one on the geometry of *outer space*, so she could learn as much as possible. He knew that Katherine had loved staring up at the stars ever since she was a little girl, and he wanted to help her reach her potential.

'PROFESSOR CLAYTOR made sure I was prepared to be a RESEARCH MATHEMATICIAN.'

In the mornings Professor Claytor would enter the classroom and take a piece of chalk from his pocket, walk up to the blackboard and continue teaching yesterday's lesson as if he had never stopped. Katherine could keep up, but she noticed that other students in the class didn't **understand** what he was teaching. She would ask questions on their behalf, realizing that they didn't have the confidence to do so. Professor Claytor felt sure that Katherine, as smart as she was, should know the answer. Finally she had to tell him that she was only asking those questions to **help** the other students.

It was clear that Katherine loved her subject and had a desire to help others understand and enjoy *complex* mathematical ideas too. This was the first sign of her strength as a *mentor and guide* to young people, which she would display throughout her life.

In 1937 Katherine graduated SUMMA CUM LAUDE. This was at a time when hardly any black people had the opportunity to achieve a high-school diploma, let alone a university degree.

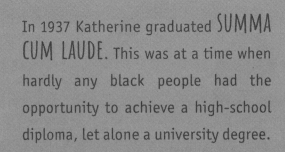

SUMMA
CUM LAUDE:
means 'with the highest distinction' – a fancy way of saying she was top of her class!

Soon after graduating, she started *teaching* at a school for black children in Marion, which is in the neighbouring state of Virginia.

WEST VIRGINIA

INSTITUTE

VIRGINIA

MARION

Life after study

One day in 1937 Katherine was on the bus from West Virginia to Virginia when it suddenly stopped after *crossing the border* between the two states. The driver ordered all the black people to move to the back. Katherine *refused to move* until the driver asked her *politely*.

This little act of **resistance** paints a picture of a woman who wouldn't let **anyone** tell her she wasn't worthy of the same rights and freedoms as white people. Katherine would go on to prove this again and again.

DID YOU KNOW?

Katherine's refusal to move from her seat came almost twenty years before Rosa Parks did the very same in Montgomery, Alabama. Rosa Parks sparked a bus boycott in 1955, and in 1956 the US Supreme Court ruled that the segregation of public transport was illegal.

Katherine taught at several different schools in Marion, but decided to stop when she *married* her first husband, James Goble. They had met when they were both students at West Virginia State College and married in 1939.

A year later she was asked by her old university to join their graduate programme in mathematics. She was excited to be back and learning again.

DID YOU KNOW?

In 1938 the US Supreme Court ruled that all states had to provide the same educational opportunities to black people as they did for white people. They could do this by setting up new universities and schools, or by allowing black people to attend institutions that had previously been only for white people.

Though Katherine jumped at the opportunity to go back to West Virginia State College, she had to leave the programme when James fell ill. By this time they had three daughters, so she returned to her teaching job to support her family, quickly getting used to the routine of school again.

DID YOU KNOW?

Katherine's daughters - Constance, Joylette and Katherine - all followed in their mum's footsteps and became teachers.

And then, a few years later, a chance conversation with a family member changed her life in ways she never could have imagined.

Making dreams a reality

One day Katherine was at a family gathering when she heard that NASA (or NACA as it was known back then) was looking for women to work at the Langley Research Center in Hampton, Virginia. Women who were maths whizzes just like Katherine were being hired to *calculate* complex mathematical problems to help planes navigate or travel through the sky from one point to another.

NACA: the National Advisory Committee for Aeronautics.

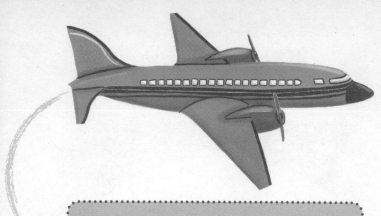

What is aeronautics?

It's the science of building machines that can fly through the sky. Aircraft can fly because they have jet engines to give them enough force to stay up in the air, and wings to keep balance, just like birds.

Katherine applied for the job – she felt like she had to! The pay was better than her teaching job, and more than anything this was her chance to study the **sky and the stars** she gazed at when she was a child.

Katherine's mother had warned her about the potential *difficulties* of working for a company with mostly white employees. But there was no stopping Katherine from taking the job when it was offered to her. She replied to her mum's warning:

'Tell them I'M COMING.'

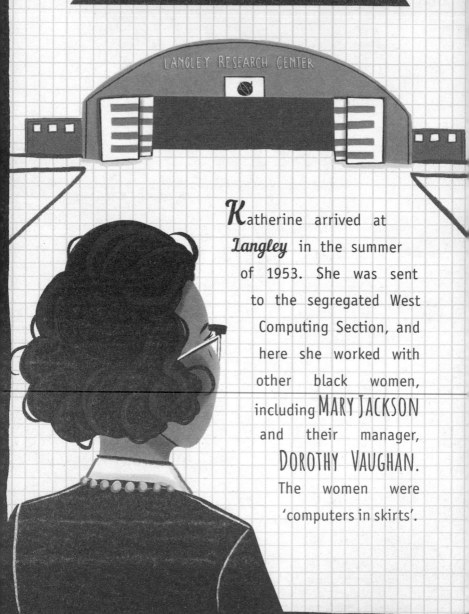

From 'computer in a skirt' to living wonder

LANGLEY RESEARCH CENTER

Katherine arrived at *Langley* in the summer of 1953. She was sent to the segregated West Computing Section, and here she worked with other black women, including MARY JACKSON and their manager, DOROTHY VAUGHAN. The women were 'computers in skirts'.

DOROTHY VAUGHAN worked with Katherine at Langley. Dorothy managed the section that Katherine was part of, becoming the first African-American woman to supervise a team at Langley.

MARY JACKSON became NASA's first black female engineer. She went on to manage both the Federal Women's Program (in the NASA Office of Equal Opportunity Programs) and the Affirmative Action Program. She worked to ensure that black women like her were hired and promoted in the organization.

The women worked in **separate rooms** from the white staff at the institute, and had to use a different toilet in a completely different building.

Katherine and her co-workers were **mathematicians**, but they were denied this title and called 'computers' because of the prejudice against them at the time. Katherine ignored this; she was there to **work**, and work she did.

'My father's advice helped. He said, "You're no better than anybody else, but nobody is better than you."'

Saving future lives

After only two weeks at Langley, Dorothy **promoted** Katherine. She spent the next four years researching and analysing aircraft MANOEUVRES.

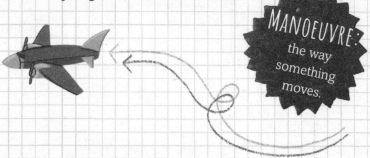

MANOEUVRE: the way something moves.

As part of her work Katherine discovered why a small propeller plane had **crashed** with no warning. She did this by studying **black boxes**, which are flight-recording devices that store information, such as the journey a plane took and sounds from the cockpit.

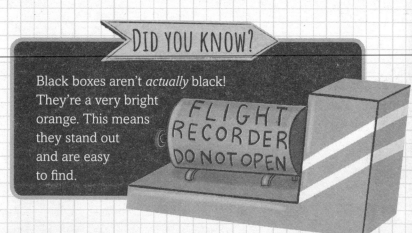

DID YOU KNOW?

Black boxes aren't *actually* black! They're a very bright orange. This means they stand out and are easy to find.

FLIGHT RECORDER DO NOT OPEN

These special metal boxes are like a treasure chest of clues, and they helped Katherine work out lots of puzzles in her early career. For instance, she found that the *flight path* of a large plane can *disturb* the air around a small plane for almost an hour after it has passed. That is what caused the first crash Katherine studied.

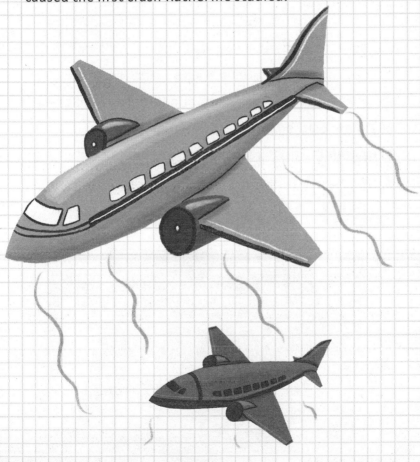

It wasn't just her skill with numbers that helped her to do well. Katherine asked lots of *questions*, wanting to know *how and why* things were the way they were. She even asked why *only men* could go to important meetings. Didn't it make sense for her to be there too, considering the essential work that she was doing?

She asked: 'Is there a law that says I can't go?' This stopped the men in their tracks. With no answer to her question, she was finally allowed to attend these meetings, once again proving that she wasn't going to let *anything* stop her from doing her job.

Three years after Katherine started at Langley, her husband James died of a brain tumour. She was a strong and *determined* woman, and despite her sadness she kept going to give her daughters the best possible life.

Making breakthroughs

1955 was a big year – for Katherine and the rest of the world. But at the time she didn't know that it was going to change her life *forever*.

On 29 July 1955 the USA told the world that it was going to launch ARTIFICIAL SATELLITES into space to orbit the Earth. This was *massive* news!

ARTIFICIAL SATELLITE: a device made by humans to orbit a planet. It sends information back to Earth about outer space to help us learn about planets, stars and much more.

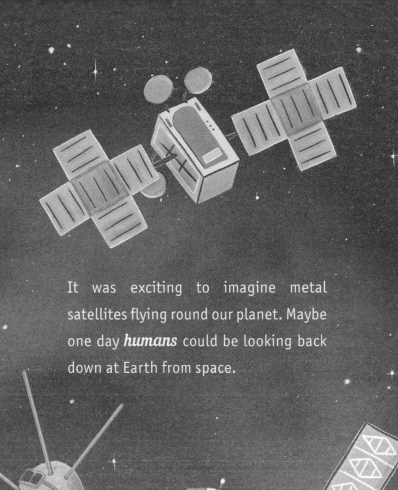

It was exciting to imagine metal satellites flying round our planet. Maybe one day *humans* could be looking back down at Earth from space.

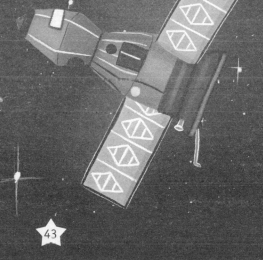

Only four days later the **USSR** announced that it too was going to launch satellites into space in the near future. Relations between the two countries grew more than a little **tense.** This started what is called **the space race**, which properly kicked off two years later.

On 4 October 1957 the USSR launched **Sputnik**, the first satellite to orbit the Earth.

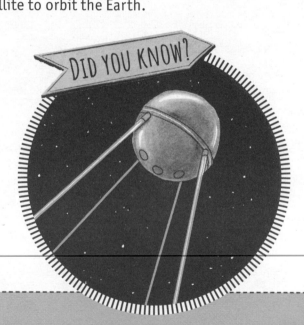

DID YOU KNOW?

Sputnik is Russian for 'traveller'. In total the satellite completed 1,440 orbits of the Earth.

It orbited the Earth for **three weeks** until its batteries eventually ran out, but it kept going for another two months before tumbling down into Earth's ATMOSPHERE. It burst into flames, crashing down to Earth as a fireball close to where it was first launched.

ATMOSPHERE:
the Earth's atmosphere is like a massive blanket. It keeps our planet warm by absorbing the sun's heat.

Next, the Russians set their sights on sending a human into space, and the man for the job was called **Yuri Gagarin**. Before he could take on this huge once-in-a-lifetime mission, he had to **train for years**. Meanwhile, the American government wasn't too happy that the Russians had aced the Sputnik mission, and so they kept trying to prove that they were bigger, better and **stronger** than the USSR. However, America had some catching up to do, and fast. While **governments** fought and experts paced up and down wondering what to do next, Katherine was working away at the **maths** needed to get people to and from space.

Not long after the launch of Sputnik, Katherine published a document that made it clear that America was ready to have a go at space travel. To make it even clearer, NACA became NASA on 29 July 1958. Now the National Aeronautics and Space Administration, it became a space agency with a *mission* to send people into Earth's ORBIT and beyond.

ORBIT:
the path an object takes around another object (like the moon around the Earth).

A year after NASA was founded, Katherine married her second husband, *Colonel James A. Johnson*, a man who saw her as the extraordinary woman she is, and loved her for it.

DID YOU KNOW?

Since NASA was launched in 1958,
it has seen astronauts orbit the Earth and travel
further still to the moon. But the agency's
plans haven't stopped there.

Space stretches for billions and billions of miles, so
there's lots more to see! NASA has sent many missions
to space, and has helped to build the *International
Space Station* in the hope that American astronauts
might return to the moon by 2020.

There are also plans to travel to Mars, and Katherine
worked on the calculations for the early research stages.
It takes many, many years for a mission to go from
an idea to the reality of space travel!

Americans and Russians in space

Sending people to space is a *gigantic* job, so where was NASA going to start? First, they found a group of ASTRONAUTS who would be the first Americans to journey into space.

WHAT ARE ASTRONAUTS?

Astronauts are specifically trained to travel beyond the Earth's atmosphere. They have to wear special spacesuits and helmets, and undertake a lot of tests to make sure they're ready for the trip.

WHAT DOES IT TAKE TO GET TO SPACE?

It wasn't just a fear of heights that could stop someone from becoming an astronaut. The MERCURY SEVEN had to pass lots of physical tests and be qualified to fly a jet aircraft and, because there was hardly any room in the early satellites, they had to be no more than 1.8 metres tall and weigh less than 82 kilograms.

THE MERCURY SEVEN

When NASA set out to find the **very first** astronauts, they met and tested 508 people. Only seven were successful. Their names were Scott Carpenter, Gordon Cooper, John Glenn, Gus Grissom, Wally (Walter) Schirra, Alan Shepard and Deke Slayton. These men came to be known as the Mercury Seven, and it was Katherine who pioneered the maths behind the success of their voyages.

DID YOU KNOW?

The seven were named 'Mercury' because the programme that took them to space was called Project Mercury – the forerunner to the Apollo moon missions.

YURI GAGARIN

Despite the efforts of the USA, it was the Russians who succeeded in sending the first person into space: in April 1961 Yuri Gagarin orbited the Earth in the *Vostok 3KA space capsule*.

VOSTOK 3KA

ALAN SHEPARD

This wouldn't stop the Americans, and they became even more determined to prove that they could keep up with the USSR. In May 1961 Alan Shepard boarded the rocket he named *Freedom 7*. He was fired up and up, beyond the atmosphere, becoming the first American in space.

UNITED STATES

FREEDOM 7

'THE EARLY TRAJECTORY WAS A PARABOLA *and it was easy to predict* WHERE IT WOULD BE AT ANY POINT.'

DID YOU KNOW?
Rockets, satellites and other spacecraft can't fly in a straight line! That's why they travel in orbits or parabolas.

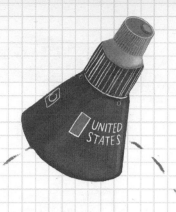

Parabolas

The path Alan
Shepard took in the rocket
was a **_parabola_**, a kind of curve
shaped like an arch. Following this,
it was easy to locate Alan as he was
whooshed above the Earth.

JOHN GLENN

Katherine soon met a man called John Glenn, who was to make his journey to space in a rocket called *Friendship 7*. By this point Katherine had already **proved** that she was a master of numbers, so John knew he could trust her completely. While he trained, Katherine worked hard *calculating* how to get him into space and back home again.

As he was to become the first American to orbit the Earth and Katherine was to become the woman who would get him there, they both had very *important* work to do.

1962 came and Friendship 7 was ready and waiting to be fired into Earth's orbit.

The mission was huge, and more than a little ***nerve-racking*** for everyone involved. NASA had lots of different experts watching John during his mission to make sure that he was safe.

Back on Earth, Katherine was running the show. There was a lot of pressure on them both! But John trusted Katherine, believing in her amazing ability to move numbers around in her brain. Before boarding the rocket, he said:

'Get the girl, check the numbers. If the numbers are good, then I'm ready to go.'

– John Glenn

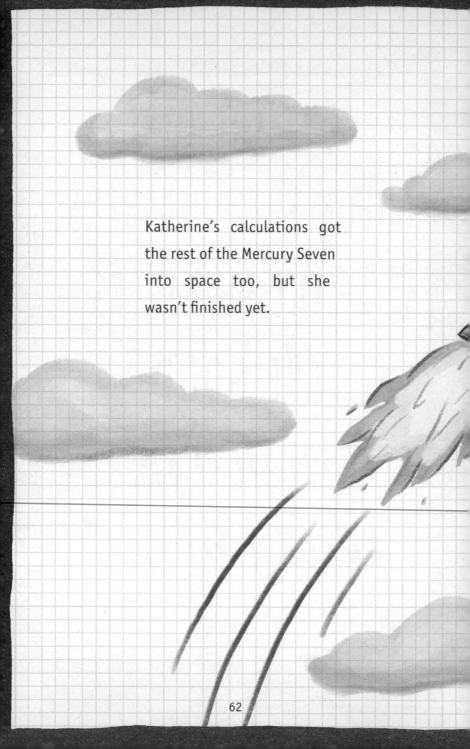

Katherine's calculations got the rest of the Mercury Seven into space too, but she wasn't finished yet.

DID YOU KNOW?

The top section of the rocket is the only part that goes into space. The remaining sections are full of fuel and drop off once the rocket reaches a certain height.

63

*T*he success of John Glenn's mission was a **huge victory** for the USA. The space race with the USSR was heating up. Ambitions now soared much higher than the Earth's orbit, and Katherine started work on a project that would be the **highlight of her career** at NASA – Apollo 11, the moon landing of 1969.

'I COMPUTED
the path
THAT WOULD
GET YOU
THERE.'

Katherine had been **researching** the maths it would take to get people to the moon, and with every breakthrough she made, the idea became more of a reality. *Finally*, in 1969, the time came.

Apollo 11 was the mission that carried Neil Armstrong, Buzz Aldrin and Michael Collins to space, and on to *the moon*.

The astronauts were launched in a rocket called Saturn V from the Kennedy Space Center in Florida on 16 July 1969.

And by ten o'clock in the morning the three men were *circling* around the Earth. At a time when most Americans were having breakfast, three humans were on their way to the moon for the first time!

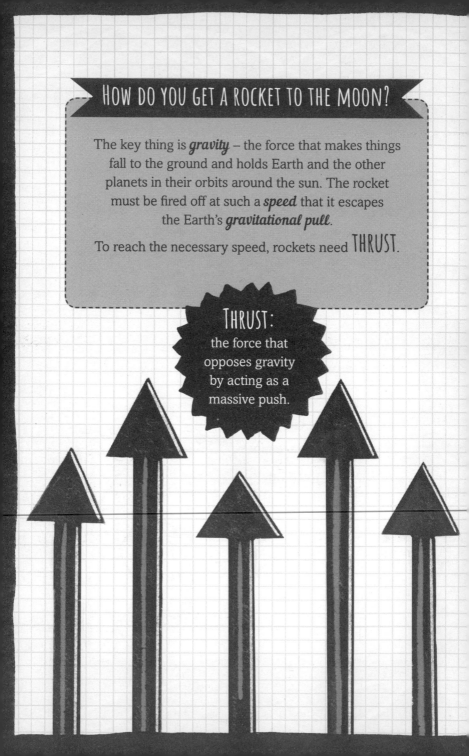

How do you get a rocket to the moon?

The key thing is *gravity* – the force that makes things fall to the ground and holds Earth and the other planets in their orbits around the sun. The rocket must be fired off at such a *speed* that it escapes the Earth's *gravitational pull*.

To reach the necessary speed, rockets need THRUST.

THRUST:
the force that opposes gravity by acting as a massive push.

In the case of rockets, the thrust is created by *explosions*. Can you imagine how huge the reactions needed to be for Saturn V's lift-off to send the rocket to the *moon*?

The explosions were *gigantic*. On that now-famous day all three men waited patiently while the rocket was preparing for lift-off. Stationed at a huge tower *hundreds* of metres tall, NASA engineers counted down the minutes before they could start the IGNITION sequence. When it started, lots and lots of *fireballs* began erupting underneath the rocket until finally it was ready to go!

IGNITION:
when something catches or is set on fire. For Saturn V lots of ignitions had to happen for it to lift off the face of the Earth.

Saturn V soared into the sky. For the launch the astronauts were in the command module **Columbia**, in specially made living quarters. Columbia was connected to **Eagle**, the smaller spacecraft that would actually land on the moon. When the rocket was high enough, both Columbia and Eagle *separated* from the rocket, zooming off towards the moon.

First steps on the moon

*T*he journey took a total of four days. The spacecraft completed one and a half orbits of the Earth and then headed towards its **destination**. Just three days later, the three men were in the moon's orbit.

Neil and Buzz clambered into Eagle and touched down on the moon's *surface* at 4:18 p.m. on 20 July 1969. After a few hours of preparation, Neil climbed down a ladder on to the lunar surface, becoming the *first person ever* to set foot on the moon.

Neil Armstrong planted the American flag as a *reminder* of who had got there first, and as an everlasting sign of what he and his team had achieved.

WHAT WAS MICHAEL COLLINS DOING?

He had the important job of steering Columbia into the perfect position so that it could reattach to Eagle and pick up Neil and Buzz for the journey home.

The moon landing was shown on live TV all over the world, with over **500 million** people watching. This is when Neil Armstrong said the famous words:

'ONE SMALL STEP
for man,
ONE GIANT LEAP
for mankind.'

It was, of course, a *huge success* for Katherine. After all, she was the one who carried out the calculations that had made the mission *possible*. It was Katherine's calculations that got them home again too.

On 21 July 1969 Neil and Buzz were ready to go home. They had *collected samples* and taken *photos*. Just as it had on Earth, the spacecraft needed to be *thrust* away from the moon at a great enough speed for them to head back to Earth.

DID YOU KNOW?

Gravity on the moon is six times weaker than gravity on Earth, so their spacecraft didn't need nearly as much thrust to get into space.

Katherine after Apollo 11

The trajectories that Katherine had calculated continued to be used for future missions. She also created **textbooks** to help students learn about **outer space**, and **maps of the stars** so astronauts could navigate safely home. In 1986, having spent **thirty-three years** working at NASA, she retired.

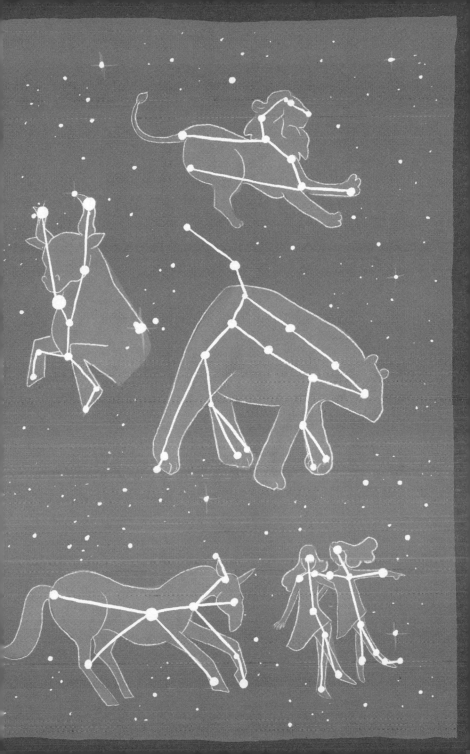

Some of the amazing things that Katherine did while she worked at NASA:

★ Contributed maths for 'Notes on Space Technology', a really important document that helped the USA plan its missions into space.

★ Became the first woman in the Flight Research Division to receive a credit as an author of a research report.

★ Made calculations that helped get the first Americans into space and Neil Armstrong and Buzz Aldrin to the moon.

★ Co-wrote twenty-six research reports.

Katherine hadn't always had the easiest time in America. She'd been *forced* to use toilets and transport separate from white people and was unable to *take advantage* of the same opportunities in education or work. She and *millions more* like her had many barriers to knock down before they could succeed. But she *did* succeed, despite the odds.

'I DON'T HAVE A FEELING OF INFERIORITY. *Never had.* I'M AS GOOD AS ANYBODY, BUT NO BETTER.'

Katherine continues to push young people to **work harder** and follow careers in science and technology. She knows how **exciting** it can be, and how your **passion** can help change the world.

DID YOU KNOW?

Katherine sang in the choir of her local church for fifty years!

So great has Katherine's *impact* been that in 2017 NASA opened the *Katherine G. Johnson* building at the Langley Research Center, where she started her groundbreaking research sixty-four years earlier.

Katherine made it easier for other black people to follow in her footsteps. This was *celebrated* in 2015 when the then-president of the United States of America, Barack Obama, awarded Katherine the

PRESIDENTIAL MEDAL OF FREEDOM.

THE PRESIDENTIAL MEDALS OF FREEDOM:

first awarded in 1963 by President John F. Kennedy for achievements in everything from art and music to fighting for civil rights.

This is the highest honour an American citizen can be given, and Katherine had more than earned it.

'In her thirty-three years at NASA Katherine was a pioneer *who broke the barriers of race and gender,* showing generations of young people that everyone can excel in math and science, *and reach for the stars.*'

– President Barack Obama

Though she never expected any fame or glory, Katherine is now getting the international *recognition* she deserves, and people know her name as well as those of Neil Armstrong and Buzz Aldrin. In 2016 a woman named MARGOT LEE SHETTERLY wrote a **book** called *Hidden Figures: The Untold Story of the African-American Women Who Helped Win the Space Race*. The book is about Katherine and her mathematics colleagues, including Dorothy Vaughan and Mary Jackson. A year later the book inspired a *film* that brought Katherine's story to life.

MARGOT LEE SHETTERLY

had learned about Katherine, and other women like her, from her father, who worked at NASA. She wanted the whole world to hear about these extraordinary women.

'WE ARE LIVING IN A PRESENT
THAT THEY WILLED
INTO EXISTENCE WITH
their pencils,
their slide rules,
their mechanical
calculating machines –
AND, OF COURSE,
their brilliant minds.'

– Margot Lee Shetterly

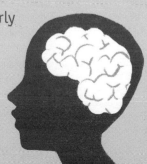

Even with people all over the world admiring her, Katherine remains **modest**. According to her, she was just doing her job.

'SHE HAD A *top-secret job*, AND WE DID NOT KNOW WHAT SHE DID, AND SHE NEVER DISCUSSED IT. *She was very humble.'*

– Laurie, Katherine's granddaughter

Now over 100 years old, Katherine lives a **quiet life** in Hampton, Virginia. She stopped working years ago, but she is still an **extraordinary woman**. In her long life she's never stopped wanting to **learn**, and she has passed this on to her children and grandchildren.

Katherine worked hard to **open doors** that were shut to her, and she did it because she knew that she had something *valuable* to contribute. The girl who loved to count didn't let anyone or anything stop her discovering and making amazing things happen.

Katherine and her story are extraordinary – because of who she is and what she's done, but also because of what we can learn from her. Her story teaches us that if we work hard at the things we love, we can succeed and reach for the stars.

TIMELINE

26 August 1918
(Women's Equality Day
in the USA)
Katherine is born.

1928
The family move
to Institute, West
Virginia.

1933
Katherine is accepted to
study at West Virginia
State College.

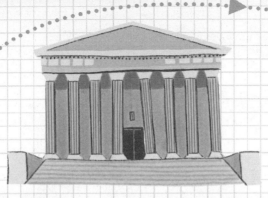

1938

The US Supreme Court rules that all states have to provide the same educational opportunities to black people as they have for white people.

1937

Katherine graduates from West Virginia State College with an honours degree in maths and French. She then starts teaching at a school for black students in Virginia.

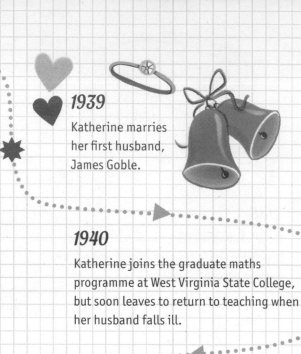

1939

Katherine marries her first husband, James Goble.

1940

Katherine joins the graduate maths programme at West Virginia State College, but soon leaves to return to teaching when her husband falls ill.

1953

Katherine starts work at the Langley Research Center at NACA.

LANGLEY RESEARCH CENTER

1956

James Goble dies
of a brain tumour.

29 July 1955

The space race begins when America
and the USSR both announce that
they will send people into space.

October 1957

The USSR launches
Sputnik, the first satellite
to orbit the Earth.

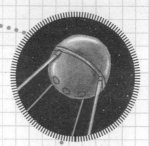

29 July 1958

NACA becomes NASA, the National
Aeronautics and Space Administration.

1959

Katherine marries her
second husband, Colonel
James A. Johnson.

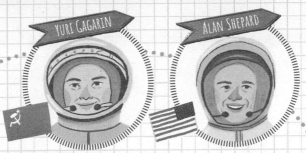

April 1961

Yuri Gagarin becomes the first person in space and the first to orbit the Earth. A month later, aided by Katherine's calculations, Alan Shepard becomes the first American in space.

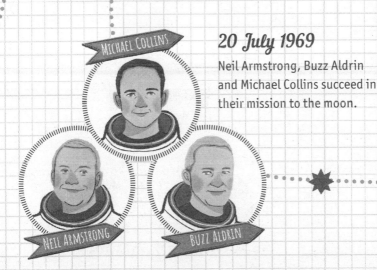

20 July 1969

Neil Armstrong, Buzz Aldrin and Michael Collins succeed in their mission to the moon.

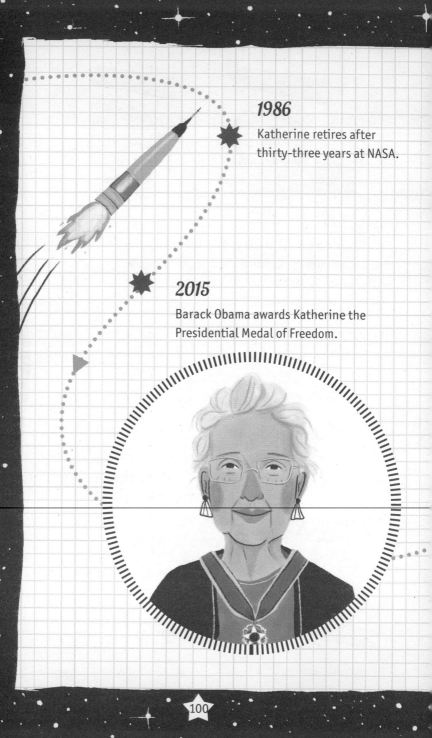

1986

Katherine retires after thirty-three years at NASA.

2015

Barack Obama awards Katherine the Presidential Medal of Freedom.

2016

Margot Lee Shetterly writes *Hidden Figures: The Untold Story of the African-American Women Who Helped Win the Space Race*.

22 September 2017

NASA opens the Katherine G. Johnson building at the Langley Research Center.

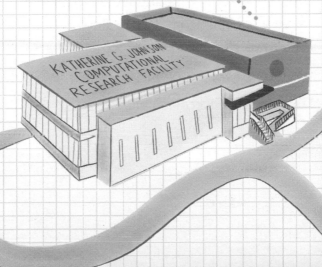

Professor Claytor was one of the people who really helped Katherine reach her full potential. How would you describe your favourite teacher? What makes them special? What adjectives would you choose to describe how great they are?

When Katherine first joined NASA she was called a 'computer in a skirt'. Do you think it was a fair title for the women who did such important work? How do you think it might feel to be called a computer?

Want to see what a parabola looks like? This is the curved path a spacecraft takes when it goes into orbit.

You can see parabolas everywhere – from bouncing balls to fountains and suspension bridges.

Index

Quote Sources

Direct quotes throughout are from the following sources:

Pages 7, 65, 83: 'Katherine Johnson Did The Math For NASA When It Counted Most' (M. Mink, investors.com, 29 December 2016)

Page 11: WHROTV interview with Katherine Johnson 25 February 2011

Page 13: 'Katherine Johnson: The Girl who Loved to Count' (NASA, 2015)

Page 15: 'The unbelievable life of the forgotten genius who turned Americans' space dreams into reality', (M. Bartels, www.businessinsider.com, 22 August 2016)

Pages 20, 23: 'Katherine Johnson: A Lifetime of STEM' (NASA, 2013)

Page 33: Katherine Johnson Biography from NASA, M. L. Shetterly

Page 37: 'NASA Pioneer Katherine Johnson Q&A' (S. Lindsey, AARP, March 2018)

Page 56: 'Mathematician Katherine Johnson at Work' (S. Loff, NASA, 25 February 2016)

Page 61: 'How three black women helped send John Glenn into orbit' (E. Helmore, *Guardian*, 11 December 2016)

Page 87: 'Honoring NASA's Katherine Johnson, STEM Pioneer' (K. Ford, Obama White House, 30 November 2015)

Page 89: 'NASA Langley's Katherine Johnson Computational Research Facility Officially Opens' (E. Gillard, NASA, 23 September 2017)

Page 90: 'The Granddaughter Of Katherine Johnson Gushes On The Hidden Figure Audiences Didn't Get To See' (Tanya A. Christian, *Essence*, 18 May 2017)

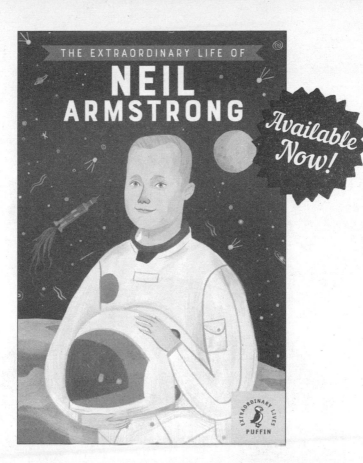

Discover the incredible story of the first man to set foot on the moon in

THE EXTRAORDINARY LIFE OF

NEIL ARMSTRONG

Keep reading for a sneak peek . . .

WHO WAS
Neil
Armstrong?

*O*n 21 July 1969, at just before four minutes to three in the morning, a man stepped off a *ladder*. Around the world 530 million people held their breath and watched a black-and-white image on boxy, old-fashioned televisions. The man was *Neil Armstrong*, commander of the Apollo 11 space mission, and at the bottom of the ladder was the *surface* of the *moon*.

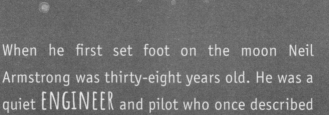

When he first set foot on the moon Neil Armstrong was thirty-eight years old. He was a quiet ENGINEER and pilot who once described himself as a 'nerd'.

Neil's step was one of the most important and extraordinary in human history. With one footstep he showed that humanity's voyages of discovery could continue out into space.

ENGINEER:
someone who designs and makes machinery.

Available Now!

Discover how one of the greatest scientists of all time changed the world with his discoveries in

*S*oon after his twenty-first birthday, Stephen Hawking was told that he had a rare disease and that he did not have long to live. He went on to live for *fifty-five* more years! He became one of the most famous and respected *scientists* and *thinkers* of our times. He also inspired *millions* of people by showing that disability does not stop you from achieving *great things* . . .

STONEHENGE

CAMBRIDGE

OXFORD   ST ALBANS

(HIGHGATE)
LONDON

ENGLAND

Stephen Hawking

was born in Oxford on 8 January 1942.

He went to Oxford University for his first degree and then studied at Cambridge. He was a scientist who tried to answer difficult questions, such as *'How did the universe begin?'* He definitely enjoyed a *challenge*.